Blessed Be

An Illustrated Walk Through A Year In The Hampshire Countryside

Written by

Lady May

Illustrated by Sarah Keen

Published by sarahNet Ltd

sarahNet Ltd, Shedfield, Hampshire SO32 2JE

First Published in the United Kingdom 2014

DISCLAIMER

All of the recipes given in this book are based upon the traditional use of the herbs they contain and in no way constitutes, nor are they intended to be used as a prescriptive format. Always seek the help and advice of a professionally trained and fully qualified herbal practitioner.

ACKNOWLEDGMENTS

I am so grateful to everyone who took the time and trouble to comment on Blessed Be and help it develop from an on line site to this gentle paperback. In particular I thank Lady May for her patience and kindness whilst this book came together. It has been an absolute pleasure to work with her. I also thank my father, Corris Keen, for his constant support and encouragement.
Thank you all; this book could not have been completed without your help.

Sarah Keen

***

'My heartfelt thanks and appreciation to - my husband, Michael and to Sarah for her unique and exquisite illustrations and for all she has given to the production of this book. I thank you both, from the very top and bottom of my heart. A dream come true, at last'.

Lady May

FOREWORD

It was the end of January 2012 and typically for the time of the year I was feeling tired and worn down by the short days that were quickly gobbled up by seemingly endless nights. Spring seemed far off and all warmth fled.

I met with Lady May for a drink. She as usual was fizzing with energy. How does she sustain this I wondered, she seems to tap into secret wells of vitality. She looks out on bleak mid-winter and finds joy. I see the same scene and worry about floods and mud and perilous journeys to work.

Lady May was surprised at my pessimism. It's all part of the cycle of nature. All is well. Everything is as it should be.

Then she announced that as this was New Year she had a New Year Resolution: she would write me a country diary for each month and, she said with touching faith in my ability, I should illustrate it.

We clinked our glasses together and agreed. Sure enough, at the end of February the first account rolled in and then March followed. Blessed Be began to unfold in front of me.

It's been a joy to illustrate Lady May's charming accounts of the seasons, but I find comfort in her account that we are not outside of nature; we have a place and a rhythm in the cycle of the year. Mankind is not necessarily an alien destructive species on this planet. We can, to adapt a phrase, Turn On our Senses, Tune In to Nature and Drop into Harmony with our environment.

When this happens we will all grow.

Blessed Be

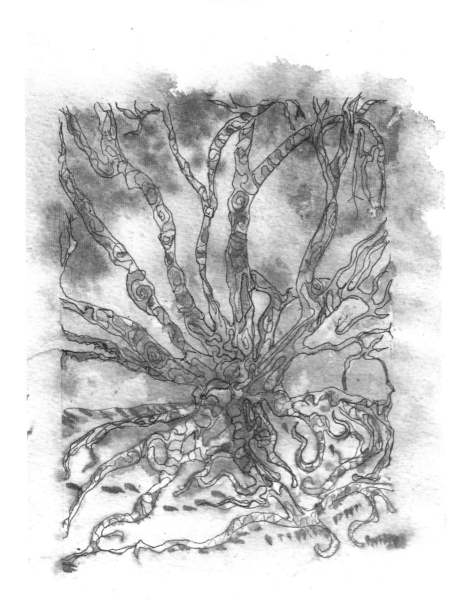

Yew Tree In Winter

FEBRUARY

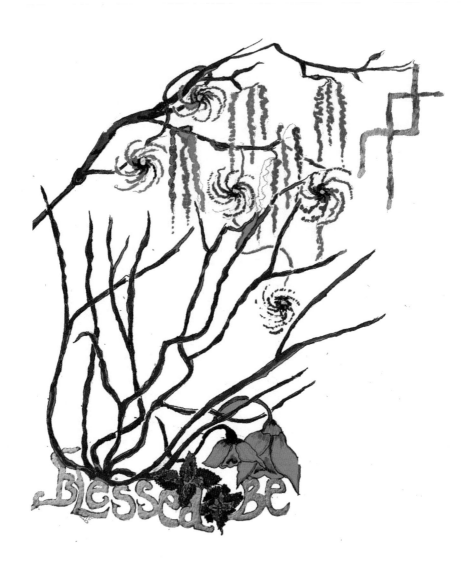

Feb 2nd Imbolg also known as Candlemas

As I wander along the quiet country lane on a crisp winter's morning, a smile begins to spread across my face. A bright beam of sunlight strikes the hedgerow awakening the sleepy flora and fauna and I know the darkness of winter is behind us.

The burgundy red spires of dogwood stems add a rich and vibrant warmth to the brown hues of the twigs and stems, striking yellow gorse lights up the way like little lamps shining brightly and clumps of Old Man's Beard drift aimlessly from branch to branch.

Bramble masks its prickly presence with a rich purple glow of arching stems and the hazel catkins dangle their luminous yellow fronds as if beckoning to come closer and listen ...

Listen to the gentle hum deep within the earth, only those who do not hear think this is a quiet time of year, quiet and still. How wrong they are; for already things are waking from the long winter slumber, shaking free from the cloak of darkness and igniting with new life.

Snowdrops, so pure, so gentle, seem to bob their heads in recognition, their inner beauty hidden deep within the capped petals. White and green, traditional colours of spring, white signalling the return of light upon the earth, light returning from the winter's darkness and resting time and green to signify the excitement of new life as buds begin to form and swell.

And there, just there, peeping out from beneath the dark womb of the earth, the very first shoots of new nettles. Dark green and succulent and already my mouth begins to water at the thought of a tasty nettle soup. Nettles, packed with vitamins and minerals help to cleanse the liver from winter's over indulgences and fortify the blood, a true spring tonic indeed. Some for the pot, some for drying and some to be made into tinctures.

So here we are, at the beginning of February and ready to celebrate the Festival of Light known as Imbolg (a Celtic word meaning ewes' milk). It is more commonly known as Candlemas. We can celebrate having survived the long hard winter passed, a time for us to close the door on its darkness and herald the coming of light and life and new beginnings all around us. Some of us mark the occasion by bringing indoors a few sprigs of hazel dripping with catkins or some beautiful delicate snowdrops. Clumps of reeds or straw may be gathered to make a Brigid's cross, a talisman that represents the quickening of life and the process of birth and re-birth. A reminder to us all, that from the death of winter comes life in spring and so the wheel turns.

Blessed Be

FEBRUARY RECIPE

February – Nettle Soup
Spring Tonic – fortifying and cleansing

25g butter
1 medium onion
2 cloves of garlic
400g potatoes, peeled and chopped
450g freshly picked nettle tops
1 litre vegetable stock
150ml double cream (for a richer, creamier version)
Salt and freshly ground black pepper to taste

Melt the butter in a large pan. Add the onion and garlic and fry for 10 minutes. Add the potatoes and nettles and stir for 2 minutes. Cover with the stock, bring to the boil and then reduce heat to simmer for a further 15 minutes. Leave to cool.

Blend the ingredients to a puree consistency, stir in the cream if desired and the seasoning. Reheat and serve.

My February Notes

February 'To Do' List

Date	Task	Date	Task
1		16	
2		17	
3		18	
4		19	
5		20	
6		21	
7		22	
8		23	
9		24	
10		25	
11		26	
12		27	
13		28	
14		29 l/y	
15			

MARCH

Spring Equinox March 21st

I awake to find the sun riding high up in the sky, a glorious welcome golden orb of warmth and light; renewed from its winter slumber to shine even brighter on the earth.

Outside, snowflakes fall softly and silently as rainbows catch their light and ride upon them proudly. All is quiet and white - so very white and pure - I think about springtime and its significance is not lost on me.

All seems covered by a blanket of stillness and yet, hidden beneath, so much is stirring.

The snow begins to melt revealing hidden treasures in the jewel like colours of gold and purple crocuses that bear their opulent heads to the warmth of the sun. Bright lemon-yellow daffodils rise majestically from slender greenery, their heads bobbing gracefully as tiny droplets fall from the petals one by one.

As I walk toward my herb beds, I tilt my face toward the sun and bathe for a moment in its energies. I know the darkness of winter is behind us now and the light really is returning.

Light from dark, leads us toward the Spring Equinox on March 21st. It is a solar festival that celebrates the return of the sun, bringing its warmth, light and fertility to land and vegetation. From this date, light prevails and wins the battle once more.

In the herb garden I delight at the surreal feather-like fingers of the Fennel just appearing from the bulb's crown. Angelica nestles cosily by its side also bearing signs of new life, as does Sage, Thyme and Rosemary. I make a mental note of the fact that they follow so closely on from the cleansing properties of nettles from the month before and now we have a parade of herbs all with a gentle, calming and restorative effect on the digestion.

The Sage, so appropriate in its appearance now, providing us with a wonderful healing gargle to ease the symptoms of sore throats so common at this time of year as the seasons change.

I tend my herbs lovingly, lost in the moment until there in the background, way off in the distance, I hear the unmistakable hammering of the woodpecker. A flock of geese fly overhead in formation and right in front of me, perched on an upturned flowerpot, a song thrush begins her mesmerising song and it's as if the world has stood still.

She starts the most beautiful orchestra of birdsong all around me, the robin, blackbird, blue tit, chaffinch and sparrow all join in filling the morning air with hope and joy and my heart melts like the snow.

Blessed Be

MARCH REMEDY

Sage Throat gargle
4 – 6 freshly picked sage leaves

Place the sage leaves into a mug and add boiling water.

Leave to steep for 15 minutes.

Strain and cool.

When cool, place 1 – 2 dessert spoons of the liquid into a separate cup and use to gargle with, three – four times a day.

Store in the fridge.

This should make enough gargle to last for a day or two. Make fresh as required.

Sing freely as desired.

My March Notes

March 'To Do' List

Date	Task	Date	Task
1		17	
2		18	
3		19	
4		20	
5		21	
6		22	
7		23	
8		24	
9		25	
10		26	
11		27	
12		28	
13		29	
14		30	
15		31	
16			

APRIL

The day is clear and I decide to take my bike and cycle through the little village to the river. On my way I see, peeping out timidly from beneath layers of fallen leaves, the delicate face of a primrose. Tall stems of cowslips push their way through protective grasses to rise majestically above the mound of green. Forsythia bursts into a beacon of golden stars as it flowers all at once and yellow is everywhere. Yellow, it is the colour of friendship, happiness and sunshine and there hangs in the air a promise of the halcyon days of summer to come.

I cycle lazily through country lanes and decide to stop by the banks of the river Test. I leave my bike and walk a while, drawn to follow the flow of the river and as I walk a pair of ducks paddle beside me curious of my intrusion.

There is movement ahead and a swan appears gliding gracefully out from amongst the rushes as if leading the parade. On the other side of the bank stands the stately silhouette of a heron, perfectly still, waiting.

I see the tiny purple flowers of Self Heal nestling in the spongy grass and the swollen pregnant-like belly of the white dead nettle. Next to them forcing their way upward are the upturned umbrella-like leaves of cleavers, 'sticky willy' as it is traditionally known. Well named indeed, as I remember the times I walked to school as a young girl, collecting my friends along the way and by the time we arrived in the playground giggling heartily, our jumpers were covered in the dangly stems. Everything smells so fresh and clean and there is a sweetness in the air.

I am stopped in my tracks by a fallen cloud of blackthorn blossom and stare at its ethereal beauty, its captivating presence luring you forward to come closer until a sudden sharp stab from one of its hidden thorns sends you reeling backward. I turn the corner and am greeted by candy floss tufts of pink cherry blossom reminding me of giant marshmallows. How sweet is nature.

I return home to find a blue tit busy building a mud door across a hole in the trunk of one of the apple trees. As I silently watch his valiant efforts I am reminded of the messages from nature at this time of year. Messages of fertility, creation, new life, new beginnings, hope, the sowing of seeds, new ideas, a time for making new plans.

My thoughts are interrupted only by the joyous sight of rabbits playing in the paddock, their white tails bobbing up and down amidst the lengthening grass. Further up the field a gathering of ewes watch over their new-born lambs as they skip and jump oblivious to the joy their presence bestows upon so many.

I peer into a wildlife pond and find it teeming with tadpoles, their funny little tails propelling them along in and out of the weed in a jagged fashion.

And as I turn to go indoors a bumble bee takes a low and lazy flight path before me along the edge of the fence and into the bushes humming gently to itself and as I step into my kitchen, I find myself smiling.

Blessed Be

APRIL REMEDY

Thyme Antiseptic Skin Lotion – ideal for Athlete's Foot and other fungal skin infections

½ cup Thyme stalks
½ cup Lavender flowers
½ cup Oregano stalks
2 cups organic white wine vinegar

Mix all of the ingredients together.

Store in a glass jar and shake vigorously every day for 2 weeks.

Strain and bottle the remaining liquid into a clean sterilised jar.

Will keep for a year or more if stored correctly.

To store – keep in a cool place away from direct sunlight.

My April Notes

April 'To Do' List

Date	Task	Date	Task
1		17	
2		18	
3		19	
4		20	
5		21	
6		22	
7		23	
8		24	
9		25	
10		26	
11		27	
12		28	
13		29	
14		30	
15			
16			

MAY

I stumble excitedly along the tiny narrow cobbled streets to arrive amidst the heady celebrations of Mayday and an amazing riot of colour.

The village maypole festooned with ribbons being tightly wound around the phallic pole. Maidens dancing joyfully in gay abandon as they duck and dive and weave their magic with each step. The air is full of excitement and energy and the mischief is palpable, left over from the night before by those who have spent the night in the woods 'a Maying'.

People line the streets waiting for the rhythmic beat of the drum and here it comes, accompanied by the haunting melody of the flute. Together they taunt us playfully as we await the arrival of the ' Obby 'Oss ' and its entourage of revellers. Laughter and merriment fill the air and the excitement is tangible to all and as the procession passes I tingle with the vibration of life and being alive and I am thankful.

Such rites are a joy to behold and if you are ever lucky enough to stumble upon such festivities, I urge you to throw caution to the wind and take part, free your spirit and enjoy the celebrations of life itself in all its forms. Laugh a little and allow yourself to live.

The festivities will carry on throughout the day so I turn and make my way back up the hill to the woods, now quiet and peaceful. I wander freely through the fabulous carpet of bluebells and let my feet bathe in the pure morning dew and as I walk contentedly, right in front of me appears a hare.

 She stands tall upon her back legs, magnificent and stares straight at me, I am mesmerised.

Without the slightest fuss, she turns and makes her way along the track in front of us and then she stops, raising one paw as if beckoning and sure enough, from behind a mound of bracken appears another hare and he joins us. All three of us continue on our way and my heart sings with joy, I cannot believe what is happening and how Blessed I am to share this moment with such mystical creatures. I stop to admire a clump of white wood anemone and the tiny flower of the wild violet next to it. A hawthorn bush now laden with white blossom stands close by and I think of the beautiful floral crowns worn by the May Queen interlaced with the bounty of colour I see before me now.

I look back but the hares have disappeared; I thank them for their time and for their presence.

Making my way back down toward the harbour a shower of hailstones descends upon us and I watch as they bounce across the cobbles like cracking popcorn. The cloud-burst passes, the glorious sun re-appears and I inhale the freshness from the dampened air.

Blessed Be

MAY REMEDY

Mint Tea

For Headaches & Fever. Aids Digestion,

Pick a few heads of fresh garden mint and place in a cup or mug.

Pour on boiling water and leave to steep for 5 minutes.

Remove the mint from the cup and when cool enough, sip the remaining liquid.

My May Notes

May 'To Do' List

Date	Task	Date	Task
1		17	
2		18	
3		19	
4		20	
5		21	
6		22	
7		23	
8		24	
9		25	
10		26	
11		27	
12		28	
13		29	
14		30	
15		31	
16			

JUNE

Midsummer Day dawns to a fanfare of birdsong against the backdrop of an early morning sky tinted with pink and grey. Walking barefoot upon the spongy mounds of moss and grasses I revel in the thought of my feet being bathed in the purity of fresh morning dew. I kneel before a great oak to scoop a handful of dew into the palms of my hands and splash my face with its invigorating coolness. As I open my eyes a flurry of elderflower petals shower me from above and stick to my wet face. I look up and am sure I hear the childlike titter of faerie folk having one last laugh before the true day dawns and they are gone.

I lift the rusty latch of my garden gate and step into a sea of blue delphiniums broken only by the tantalising bejewelled swords of lupins. The gate swings shut, creaking as it goes.

The sun rises bringing with it the warmth of the day and all around me wakens. I sit in my chair under the apple tree and watch the parents of blue tit chicks flying frantically back and forth as they try to satisfy their hungry brood.

A fox jumps the fence at the bottom of the garden and saunters casually along the pebble path to the pond where he stops to take a drink. I watch whilst he preens himself, his beautiful auburn fur glistening like treacle in the sunlight. He stretches lazily, gives a big yawn and then turns and saunters back the way he came leaving only his smell behind him.

I notice the glistening whiteness of delicate daisies nestling in the grass and find myself making daisy chains for the little girls who live next door. I hang them on the handle bars of the bicycles they ride to school. A present from the fairies.

Time to pick some fresh flowers for my kitchen table and as I place them gently, one by one into my wicker basket the air is filled with the heady aroma of an English summer.

An apple falls from the tree and I hear its familiar 'thud' as it hits the ground knocking several others off their branches during its descent. Ah yes, June drop. All around the base of the tree lay tiny apples, the weak ones falling to make way for the strongest to survive and I stop to think how selfless and giving nature truly is.

I lean forward to pick a luscious strawberry, the month of June in a fruit and I notice a blackbird watching me patiently from the top of the blueberry bush. Do not worry, little bird, there is plenty left for you.

As I turn to go indoors my skirt catches on the thorns of a rose bush that scratch me and draw blood as I struggle to free myself. Those faerie folk again and I look around me just one more time, are they watching? In complete defiance, I cup a beautiful bloom into both hands and draw it slowly toward me savouring the moment when this treasure yields its rich perfume and I am enchanted.

Making my way back up the garden path I stop suddenly, there is something missing, the high pitched cheeping of the baby blue tits, all is quiet. Very slowly I make my way to the apple tree and peep inside the nest. It is empty, they have flown and so the wheel turns.

Blessed Be

JUNE RECIPE

Elderflower Cordial - Summer in a cup

Anti-viral properties, helps fight colds and flu – traditionally drunk hot
for those summer colds

25 elderflower heads
3 un-waxed lemons finely grated zest
1 un-waxed orange finely grated zest, save their juice
1kg sugar
1 heaped tsp citric acid (optional)

Tap the flower heads to remove any insects.

Place the flower heads in a large bowl with the zest of the lemons and
the orange.

In a separate pan bring 1.5 litres water to the boil and pour over the
elderflower heads and the lemon and orange zest. Cover and leave over
night to infuse.

Strain the liquid through a clean muslin bag and pour into a saucepan.
Add the sugar, citrus juice – about 150 mls – and the citric acid if used.
Heat gently until the sugar has dissolved, bring to simmer and cook for a
couple of minutes.

Using a funnel, pour the hot liquid into clean, sterilised bottles and
secure the lid.

Leave to cool and enjoy.

My June Notes

June 'To Do' List

Date	Task	Date	Task
1		17	
2		18	
3		19	
4		20	
5		21	
6		22	
7		23	
8		24	
9		25	
10		26	
11		27	
12		28	
13		29	
14		30	
15			
16			

JULY

Reclining lazily upon my sunbed drifting in and out of a relaxing daydream I am disturbed by the low drone of approaching bees. Thousands of them grouped together in a tight black cloud that hovers and then hangs below the branch of a tree. I sit up and stare in awe at the sight before me, half afraid to move and yet transfixed at the same time. The swarm swirls and sways suddenly, the shape changing to an arrow head as if leading the way and slowly, as if being sucked by a vacuum, they drift away and are gone.

Too content to get up I lie back and stare upon the blue sky of summer. The intricate weave of delicate gossamer clouds forming random shapes that evolve and then vaporise before our very eyes. Imagination stirs, a unicorn appears before me and I am transported to another place and another mystical, magical time. He drifts on by rising higher into the sea of blue becoming ever smaller until he disappears in a puff.

Swallows dip and dive chirruping busily as they go, their forked tail feathers distinct as they fly overhead. Higher, oh so much higher in the sky a buzzard rides the thermals playfully. Perfect peace shattered suddenly by the raucous squawking of angry rooks defending their territory from a marauding magpie.

 I take a stroll through my garden and out into the field beyond. The once lush green grass now lying cut and golden yellow crackles beneath my footsteps. Bales of hay like giant Swiss rolls dot the landscape waiting to be collected by the big blue tractor stopped under the shade of the trees. I wave to the farmer sitting on one of the giant tyres swinging his legs and eating his lunch. He waves back and all is well.

Butterflies flit silently by, coming to rest upon an old wooden cart wheel, their open wings revealing beautiful colours and patterns and just as I get near enough to take a closer look, they snap them shut as if teasing me playfully.

I walk alongside the wild margin feasting in the riot of colour laid before me, crimson poppies, purple thistle, pink mallow, white yarrow, yellow hawkweed and the pastel blues of chicory and cornflower, nature's own palette. The air is filled with the vintage scents of meadowsweet, honeysuckle and sweet cicely and I am in a state of sensory overload.

A wind whips up from nowhere and the rustling leaves begin their secret symphony, I stop and listen to its haunting melody. Plants and branches bend and sway revealing the hidden jewel of silver colour on the underside leaves of the motherwort

Above me a cherry tree heavily laden with dark blood red fruits waves it's tempting bounty and will not be ignored. I hop over the fence and pluck a small bunch of the rich sumptuous fruit and as I do so a dog rose scratches my arm. I smile defiantly, a small price to pay for the taste of summer.

Blessed Be

JULY REMEDY

Meadowsweet – Queen of the Meadows

Anti – inflammatory and calming properties - relief of aching joints and
muscles – calming of gastric complaints such as gastritis, indigestion,
heartburn

Pick a few fresh flower heads and make into a tea with boiling water.
When cool enough, drink as an infusion or use as a compress.

To make a compress - soak a piece of thin cotton cloth in a strong, hot
infusion. When it is cool enough, apply to joints. Leave for a few minutes,
then refresh.

You can do this two or three times a day

My July Notes

July 'To Do' List

Date	Task	Date	Task
1		17	
2		18	
3		19	
4		20	
5		21	
6		22	
7		23	
8		24	
9		25	
10		26	
11		27	
12		28	
13		29	
14		30	
15		31	
16			

AUGUST

ugust, the month of holidays and harvest, a time to sit back, rest and relax and enjoy the fruits of our labours. A time for friends and families to be together, to re-connect, a time to laugh and play and enjoy each other and all that we have. A time for quiet contemplation and thankfulness.

Something moves in my garden pond and a frog rests upon a lily pad, his throat pulsing like a beating heart and such is the rhythm of life.

Butterflies, bees and dragonflies hover and flutter between the flowers, drinking deeply from the funnels of nectar laden petals. I watch this spectacle unfold before me, an interwoven symphony of dance and psychedelic colour, there for the taking and a pure joy to behold.

I stroll across the field toward the village green to join in the festivities of a summer fete and am joined by a squirrel, who bobs happily alongside me. All of a sudden, he darts off to the left heading for a cluster of heavily laden hazelnut trees. I stop and watch for a while as he carefully inspects each bright green feathery pocket holding the juicy, plump, young hazelnut he so longs to devour.

I look around me and notice how the tiny pink faces of blackberry blossom and elegant tall spires of bright yellow agrimony light up the dappled shade. Arching branches of the buddleia bush, dripping with their purple fingers as if pointing the way – the way to where I wonder? I arrive at the green where multi-coloured bunting adorns each stall, flapping lazily in the gentle breeze as if inviting you to come closer and stare upon its wares. Home - made treats of jams, pickles, chutneys and cake, oh, those wonderful cakes. Full of naughtiness, I cannot resist their temptation and load my basket with these guilty secrets, my mouth watering at the mere thought of just how good they will taste.

Shrieks of laughter fill the air as another ball strikes the button and the ducking stool releases some poor soul into the cool clear waters of the tank beneath them.

I hear the 'click' of ball upon a willow bat, the cricket match has begun. Men in their crisp whites, play the game as if in slow motion and I decide to sit awhile and watch. Refreshments are set upon a nearby table displaying the plates of cucumber sandwiches, Victoria sponge and jugs of traditional lemonade. An old urn bubbles and hisses as it boils and a lady in a pretty floral linen dress turns the tap, releasing the water into a china tea pot. I watch as she stirs the tea three times, replaces the lid and covers the pot with a cosy, citrus notes of bergamot waft my way, ah, yes, of course, Earl Grey.

I close my eyes, hear the umpire call 'Out' and the slow rhythmic ripple of applause leads me into a gentle slumber.

Blessed Be

AUGUST REMEDY

Lavender

Calming, soothing, relieves a headache

Place 2 or 3 heads of fresh lavender flowers into a cup and pour on boiling water.

Leave to steep for 5 minutes then strain and drink as an infusion.

To relieve headache or stress - soak a cotton handkerchief or piece of thin cotton material in a stronger, cool solution of the above infusion and apply to forehead. Rest and relax. Refresh as required.

My August Notes

August 'To Do' List

1		17	
2		18	
3		19	
4		20	
5		21	
6		22	
7		23	
8		24	
9		25	
10		26	
11		27	
12		28	
13		29	
14		30	
15		31	
16			

SEPTEMBER

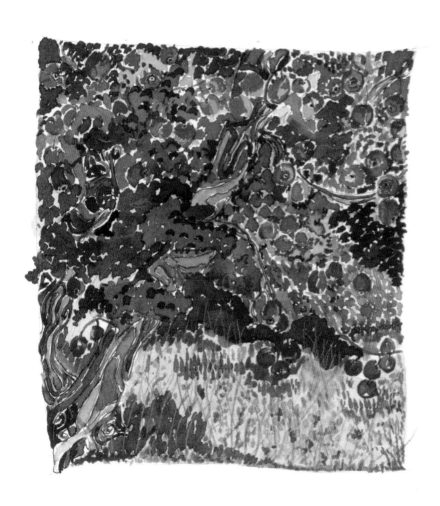

I awake to the bright sunshine of an early September morning and as I yawn and stretch ready to start the day, a chill in the air makes me shudder. Ah yes, the sun is still shining, but there is a definite reminder that the seasons are about to change. I pull back the curtains to chastise the crows who so noisily woke me and am greeted by an opaque film of condensation upon the window. Autumn is here.

I trundle toward the wooden gate at the bottom of my garden swinging my basket in eager anticipation of the bounty I am about fill it with. Big red juicy hawthorn berries beckon me enticingly and I think of the tincture I will make with them, good for the heart and the soul and my stock for the coming year. Huge plump orangey rose hips lay in wait by their side and my mouth waters at the thought of the sweet, sticky syrup they will become. I add huge purple berries from the elder tree and my arsenal of herbal remedies, ready to beat the winter blues is nearly complete.

Lavender-pink wands of loosestrife wave me on by as I continue my medicinal harvest and I notice how the branches are drooping from the drought of a long hot summer.

Geese fly in formation overhead and I marvel at the sight, like a spear piercing the blue sky, intent on its target, home they fly.

I trip and stumble and giggle to myself as I look down to find the empty shells of acorns strewn all around me, evidence indeed that I am not the only one on a mission to fill my larder. Little holes in the ground where squirrels have been busily hiding their nuts and others have been digging them up.

And there, just there, I spot a most perfect ring of tiny mushrooms, hundreds of them just crowning above the blades of grass.

I return to my garden to pick the Bramley apples that have fallen to the ground and on my way a handful of blackberries fall into my basket. A crumble is in the making.

As I bend to gather the apples I notice how the lawn is covered with tiny hammocks of cobwebs all glistening in the early sun, rocking gently on the breeze. I hail to the fairy folk who have slept there.

Cobwebs everywhere hanging from branches and twigs, the handle of the spade I left in the flower bed, from flower to flower, everywhere, cobwebs. They trap the early morning light in a canvas of magical crystal like artwork and I am drawn closer, enchanted by their magic. So pure. So fragile.

I prepare the apples for the crumble and marvel at how they can transform from firm, thick slices to powdery fluffy puree in an instant, just as you turn your back for a moment to investigate something that moves just out of vision on the wall above the Aga.

It is a spider, a big dark brown spider like the one I saw last night gliding across the carpet toward the log pile in the corner of the hearth. Welcome spider, come on in, we will share the warmth of the hearth.

Blessed Be

SEPTEMBER REMEDY

Calendula (Marigold) ointment
Antiseptic ointment for cuts, grazes, burns, stings, boils, bites

60g dried calendula flower heads
500mls sweet almond oil

Pour oil in to top section of bain-marie and add flower-heads

Add water to lower half of bain-marie

Bring to boil and then reduce to simmer

Simmer gently for 2 hours

Leave to cool and soak overnight

Strain and thicken with beeswax

Gently heat the strained calendula oil, remove from heat

Add beeswax, bit by bit – approx. 30g until it melts and begins to set

Pour into clean, sterilised jars, lid off, but covered and leave till cold

Put on lids and store.

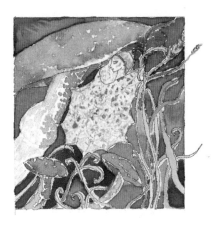

My September Notes

September 'To Do' List

1		17	
2		18	
3		19	
4		20	
5		21	
6		22	
7		23	
8		24	
9		25	
10		26	
11		27	
12		28	
13		29	
14		30	
15		31	
16			

OCTOBER

I am walking across the field toward the lane, the morning lit with the kiss of bright autumnal sunshine. Blue skies above and the busy chatter of birdsong to accompany me and my heart sings. Leaves tumble before me as they are whipped into a frenzy by the wind, twisting and twirling they weave their acrobatic dance and I am caught in their swirling vortex. I pull my coat tightly around me and hang on to my scarf as I push my way into the shelter of the woods beyond.

The trees continue their whispering above me as they bend and sway. Leaves cascade to the ground like confetti and crackle beneath my feet. I stop to admire the richness of the autumnal palette and the warmth in the hues of golden browns and orange, dotted with the ruby jewels of crab apples. My mind and body bathe in the delicious, sumptuous comfort of this autumnal offering, like slipping into a warm vat of honeyed treacle.

My path continues on through the woods and I notice the field, once full of corn, now lies flattened from the harvest. Just the odd tower of corn left, here and there for the animals to feed upon. Deep furrows filled with dewy mud and all is still and resting and I am reminded this is as it should be.

Autumn, a time of harvesting and gathering for us all, in preparation for the coming winter. A time of rest and reflection. A time to congratulate ourselves on all that we have achieved and let go of all that we have not. The end of October, a time when the veil between the worlds is at its thinnest and we are reminded of the fragility of life.

I inhale deeply and fill my lungs with the musky scent of rotting vegetation, death and decay and yet through this process new life will burst forth in the Spring and so the wheel turns.

I carry on through the woods and out into the lane, my every step watched by the beady eyes of the wizened blackberries from the once luscious fruit of the bramble.

I cut across the bridle path and am soon joined by the horses in the field as they come to greet me. Their long slender necks reach over the fence toward my coat pocket, nudging me eagerly. I reach into my pocket and withdraw an apple for each of them, they nod in thanks as they lean across and take them gently.

From out of nowhere strikes a fearsome wind lifting the horse's manes into a billowing spectre of blackness. They snort and neigh and rise defiantly upon their back legs, turn and gallop off across the field, kicking and rising as they go.

I hurry back toward my cottage taking a short cut through the paddock, over the fence and into my back garden hardly able to battle the strength of the wind and then, just as suddenly as it had started, it stops and all is so eerily still. I hear the call of a crow nearby and look up to see it perched upon a bare branch of the oak tree and as I pass, he looks down toward me and whispers, 'storm coming, storm'.

I gather my pumpkin sitting by the back door and carry it in to the kitchen closing the door behind me and I know the crow is right, 'storm coming, storm'.

Blessed Be

OCTOBER REMEDY

Elderberry Rob

Soothes coughs, sore throats and bronchial infections –

powerful anti-viral

450g fresh elderberries

450g brown sugar

Strip the berries from their stems, wash and crush them

Bring them slowly to the boil with the sugar and simmer until they reach

a syrup consistency

Pass through a sieve and bottle up in to clean, sterilised, air-tight bottles.

Serve diluted with hot water.

My October Notes

October 'To Do' List

1		17	
2		18	
3		19	
4		20	
5		21	
6		22	
7		23	
8		24	
9		25	
10		26	
11		27	
12		28	
13		29	
14		30	
15		31	
16			

NOVEMBER

Log burner lit and slippers ready warming, I put on my coat and step out into the fading light of a November afternoon. The cold air bites my nose and I pull my hat down further over my ears and head off up the lane. The days have been bright with winter sunshine, but the blue of the sky has somehow lost its vibrancy giving way to more sleepy, muted tones with a touch of greyness about them. But, at this time of day, sunset, the skies are aglow with the fiery palettes of dried oranges, deep soulful amber and blood reds.

I wend my way along the lane and turn toward the woods where I am met with a veil of tumbling brambles hung from the hedgerow like the dripping architecture of a gothic cathedral.

In an instant I am cocooned in a swirl of leaves blown from their branches and whipped into an encircling frenzy by the wind. I struggle to pull my collar up, tuck my scarf in and hold on to my hat. What a blessing to be surrounded by such colour, such energy and yet in all the warmth of the shedding colours of autumn, I feel the chill of winter.

Glancing up at the heavy skies filled with thick grey and white clouds I notice the bare skeletons of trees standing like menacing black silhouettes against the night sky.

I am startled by the sound of rustling bushes as a lone pigeon takes flight and disturbs a brace of pheasants who have been feeding nearby. They scurry across the bridleway squawking their unmistakable squawk as they try to flee the unknown predator. I hear a gunshot and then another and I understand their fear. Perched on the top rung of the farm gate, sit a row of blackbirds all in a line like skittles. One by one they fly back and forth across the lane and into the hedgerow carefully selecting the last of the autumn berries and I stop to watch awhile.

They are joined by a pair of blue tits, then sparrows, then a robin. A pile of oak leaves starts to rise upward in front of me and out from underneath pops the inquisitive twitching snout of a hedgehog. Sidling alongside the hedge appears the farmer's horse, he stretches his head to reach over the gate and nods as if bidding a greeting.

It's beginning to look like an animal's tea party and then, just as I turn to leave and as if by magic, we are graced with the exquisite presence of a roe deer. So daintily she bows her head to graze and, feeling like an intruder, I quietly withdraw and leave them to feed in peace.

I cross the field heading home and spot the distinctive heads of teasels standing tall and proud amongst the failing hawthorn. Such a curious plant; the large dark bulbous head full of prickles born upon such pale and fragile stems, leaves withered and curled like the open fanlike fins of a Komodo dragon. A sleeping dragon resting to regain his strength just as we need to at this time of year, as nature does, so must we follow in all things.

Blessed Be

NOVEMBER REMEDY

Rosehip syrup -to boost the immune system.
Rich in vitamin C
250g fresh soft rosehips
1 cinnamon stick (optional)
500ml water
125g brown sugar

Crush the rosehips slightly and place in a pan.

Add the cinnamon stick and water

Bring to a simmer and leave uncovered, simmering gently

for 20 minutes

Strain, then add the same amount of sugar as there is liquid (about 125g)

Stir until the sugar dissolves completely, then bring to the boil, reduce to

simmer for a further 10 minutes

Cool and filter into clean, sterilised bottles.

This will keep un-opened for up to a year.

My November Notes

November 'To Do' List

1		17	
2		18	
3		19	
4		20	
5		21	
6		22	
7		23	
8		24	
9		25	
10		26	
11		27	
12		28	
13		29	
14		30	
15			
16			

DECEMBER

It is December, mid-winter and the landscape has been stripped bare. Standing shy and naked its vulnerability masking the powerful forces of Nature that lie within.

I am out collecting pine cones to help kindle my log fire and as I bend to fill my basket the heady scent of the tree reminds me of all things Yule. Winter Solstice will soon be here heralding the return of the sun as minute by minute, each day, the light returns and with it hope for all things.

Holly bushes bear their fruit of bright red berries and the birds are feasting well. Mistletoe hangs heavily high up in the branches of the apple trees waiting to catch a kiss and I smile at the merriment of the season to come.

I lean against the trunk of a magnificent yew and as I wonder at the darkness of its tiny green leaves I begin to feel its heartbeat, so I close my eyes and just for a moment, we are as one.

I am woken from the moment by the seductive scent of jasmine wafting in my direction and I move to find its whereabouts. It is coming from a large Mahonia bush and as I lean forward to smell the bright yellow flowers I am startled by a lone bee, busy taking nectar from the long deep funnels of the petals. A mild winter indeed. I notice, in stark contrast to this giant of a bush before me, the gentle arching branches of a bodnantense 'Dawn'. Tiny tufts of fragile white flowers laced with baby pink edging, hanging in mid- air and like their gentle presence, they hold the most delicate of apple blossom scent.

A heavy mist rolls in advancing quickly upon the marshes like a silent gliding spectre and all around me takes on an eerie presence. I hurry back home and notice a strange coldness about me, cold and damp the air becomes and I notice an unfamiliar greyness lurking in the clouds above and I shudder.

Houses bear the distinct yellow glow of light as night begins to fall and people begin to draw their curtains, but not all the way across as is usual at this time of year. A tiny gap is left to reveal the Christmas tree adorned with colourful lights that sparkle and twinkle playfully as if winking as I pass.

A trail of smoke rises lazily from each chimney, tall and straight and high into the sky and I can smell the sweetness of the pine and oak logs as they burn.

Glad to be safely home and in the warm I delight in the fresh citrus smells of the oranges, lemons and limes drying on the hearth ready for decorations. Cinnamon sticks tied in small bundles with red ribbon release their warming fragrance and I delight in the unmistakable smells of Yule.

Mince pies and mulled wine warming on the stove ready to greet the first guests of this festive season and I ponder momentarily on the simple message of this time of year – Peace and Goodwill to all men.

Blessed Be

DECEMBER REMEDY

Lip balm: to protect and nourish your lips from the harsh winter weather

1 tsp beeswax

1 tsp coconut oil or cocoa butter

2tsp almond oil

2 drops essential oil

Put the beeswax, cocoa butter or coconut oil and almond oil into a Pyrex glass bowl

Heat over a pan over boiling water until the beeswax melts

To test the mixture to see if it is thick enough to set – chill a metal spoon in the fridge for a while – remove when it has frosted over or is cool to the touch – dip into the melted mixture and drop a small amount on to the back of your hand – roll it around with your finger – if it is too runny add a little more beeswax – if it is too hard add more of the almond oil

When you have a consistency you are happy with, allow it to cool slightly without setting and add the essential oil of your choice. Peppermint essential oil always goes well in to a lip balm, but rose or geranium is nice too.

Pour into a clean, sterilised jar and leave to set.

My December Notes

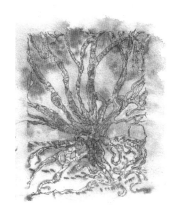

December 'To Do' List

#		#	
1		17	
2		18	
3		19	
4		20	
5		21	
6		22	
7		23	
8		24	
9		25	
10		26	
11		27	
12		28	
13		29	
14		30	
15		31	
16			

JANUARY

T he crow was right, the storm did come and then it just kept on coming. Since the end of last month and for many weeks now harsh weather conditions have re-written this island's coastlines. Rainfall, the likes of which have not been seen for more than a century, leaves the countryside drowning and submerged in its deluge.

Swollen rivers burst their banks and advance across the land engulfing everything in their path, time and time again with the rising tides. A brief respite, then the tide turns and the waters rise once more, such is the ebb and flow of life.

Coastlines are changed forever as once famous landmarks are beaten down, swallowed up and swept away by the sea, lost for all time.

Animals are taken by surprise as the swirling waters lap at their feet and they turn to run, but many are trapped by the relentless rising floods and look to farmers for rescue.

The Isle of Avalon returns and we catch a glimpse of Arthurian Somerset once more revealed and the Lakes and the scenes are set as they once were. Perhaps then, all is not just legend and fantasy.

My mind returns to the scenery around my own village and I notice how the pattern is repeated here. Where once there were fields, filled with sheep and horses, swans and ducks now swim. Seagulls perch upon fence posts jutting out above the sunken landscape, stretched across the scenery like a string of luminescent pearls. Yet in all this wet and coldness a glimmer of hope and warmth for those who see.

Rich, sumptuous colours of red and green and gold, beam like a beacon of hope from the plumage of a male pheasant as he is lit by the light of early morning sun.

Ivy vines proudly display their plump clusters of black berries like an Auntie's brooch. The silver birch tree stands proud and tall, her bare branches draping elegantly like delicate curtains opening to reveal curling bark peeling back to reveal shiny white new growth.

Tiny green shoots of the first spring bulbs begin to appear amongst the hedgerow and in gardens and the very first signs of new buds show themselves on the twigs of bushes and trees.

Wildlife tentatively re-appears. Animals slowly wake from their winter slumber; deciding whether it is time to start the cycle of life once more, or should they return to their cosy, warm nests for a little longer? It has been unusually mild for winter, but oh so wet.

The rains come and the floods keep coming, land is washed away from beneath our feet, destabilising our very existence. Foundations crumble and buildings tumble, communities rally, nature speaks to us all; let us listen and feel hope.

The previous years' warm weather had left river beds parched, cracked and reservoirs very low; we were in drought. Now the waters have come, nature is simply addressing the balance, balance in all things and all around me birds tweet , chirrup and sing beautifully and all is well.

Blessed Be

JANUARY REMEDY

Onion and brown sugar cough syrup

To soothe a tickly cough

1 large white strong onion

Sprinkling of brown sugar

Finely chop the onion and put into a bowl

Sprinkle over generously with the brown sugar

Cover and leave overnight in a warm room

In the morning, mash the onion and sugar mix and strain the juice into a

clean, sterilised bottle.

Take a teaspoon of the liquid up to four times a day.

Store in the fridge and make fresh as required.

My January Notes

January 'To Do' List

1		17	
2		18	
3		19	
4		20	
5		21	
6		22	
7		23	
8		24	
9		25	
10		26	
11		27	
12		28	
13		29	
14		30	
15		31	
16			

ABOUT THE AUTHOR

Lady May lives and works in the beautiful English Hampshire Countryside. She is a qualified herbalist and holds a diploma in Botano-Therapy (DBTh). She follows a way of life that has been passed down through her family for generations. She has taken the traditional three degrees of the Craft to become a High Priestess and is still learning.

Lady May knows she has been Blessed and greatly honoured at having been taught and mentored by some of the country's oldest, wisest Elders and followers of the Craft: Witchcraft in its truest sense as it has been practised for thousands of years, with the greatest respect for all living things.

ABOUT THE ILLUSTRATOR

Sarah Keen ran her own IT Company for almost 20 years. In 2013 she qualified with an M.A (Dist) in creative and critical writing at Winchester University, England. Following this she published her own collection of short stories for Kindle: **Runa's Ghost & Other Stories.**

She was then fortunate enough to meet Lady May and illustrate Blessed Be. All her drawings for Blessed Be are based on Hampshire's plant and wildlife.

Sarah uses pen, ink and watercolour to create her designs.

For more information please see www.sarahnet.co.uk

Please be aware that the picture of the Fox was inspired by Thorburn's glorious study and the rose with butterflies is a tribute to Richard Dadd's work; he too saw a landscape with spirits.

FURTHER INFORMATION

If you have enjoyed the illustrations in this book, please be aware many of them are for sale as diaries, calendars, prints and cards.

Blessed Be & ***Runa's Ghost*** are also available for your Kindle

To find out more about our complete range of books and products, please visit:

Website: www.sarahnet.co.uk

Facebook: Sarahnet Ltd

Twitter: #enchantedhampshire

Made in the USA
Charleston, SC
27 July 2015